An Interview with Nicolas Darvas

1974

An Interview With Nicolas Darvas 1974

INTERVIEWER: Hi, Nic. It's a pleasure to meet you in person. Thank you for agreeing to do this interview. Welcome, and please do feel comfortable.

NIC: Thanks for having me, and it's always my pleasure to discuss stocks and the stock market.

INTERVIEWER: Nic, would you mind if we get right down to talking about the stock markets? I can't wait to pick your brains on this subject. In fact, I've been waiting for many years to do this.

NIC: Sure. That's what I am here for.

INTERVIEWER: OK. After your amazing success in the late 1950s and after publishing "How I Made $2 Million in the Stock Market," how did life change for you?

NIC: It was an amazing period in my life. I went from $25,000, which was everything I had at the time, to a multi-millionaire in quite short length of time. But I was amazed at the publicity I received, that there was such a big interest in a solo stock trader. Then the success of my book was another major accomplishment in my life. It sold over 400,000 copies in the first year, you know. Sure, I was much richer than I dreamed I ever would be by 1960, but my life never changed. I carried on dancing and investing. I was able to buy more properties throughout the world with my financial success. For that I was grateful. As a person, it never changed me one bit.

INTERVIEWER: Glad to hear it, Nic. I got that impression. You seem a very sincere, down-to-earth guy. Do you think this attitude helped you succeed in the stock market?

NIC: Maybe it's not for me to say. I never got too down about losses. It never bothered me if I was out of the market for months at a time. And because my system dictated when I got out of a winning stock, I never got anxious or excited about those winnings. Looking back, I suppose it was quite remarkable how I could go from $25,000 to over $2 million with such calmness. That's me.

After the massive success in the late 1950s, I took a portion of my profits out of the stock market and invested in property. I felt there would be no point of great success if I didn't see something tangible for it. After that, I felt like I was merely participating in a game. If I followed the rules I won money. When I broke them I lost. My challenge was following the rules.

INTERVIEWER: So you admit to still making mistakes in the stock market?

NIC: Of course I do. It's very hard not to try and cut corners even when it's your own ultra money making method. Occasionally I get swayed, break the rules, lose money; but it isn't very often these days.

INTERVIEWER: What's the biggest

question you always get asked when traders find out you are Nicolas Darvas?

NIC: That's easy. Can I have your autograph and can you borrow me some money?

INTERVIEWER: Ha, ha. Really?
NIC: No. Just kidding you. Hmm... The two most asked questions I get? Let's think. They would probably be...

1) Have the markets changed?

2) Will you teach me how to trade?

INTERVIEWER: OK, Nic, can you answer those two questions for us?

NIC: Sure. First off, "Have the markets changed?" In short: no. You see, the markets are simply human emotion reflected in dollars. People really need to get this into their heads. It's not about logic, results, mathematics, but emotion. When emotion and logic collide, emotion will always come out ahead. The way I traded in the 1950s and made such fantastic money was simply the same method Livermore and Barauech traded before me. I traded the same way right the way through the 1960s and 1970s. And I am certain it will be the same going into the year 2000. It's all about riding huge waves of emotion to the maximum. The big money is made from these moves. It's crazy. But we are only human.

But having said that, while the method does stay successful, the mechanics of trading that method have and do change. As more and more traders adopt one method of entering and exiting these stocks, the floor traders then see easy pickings as they fleece the crowd. My entry in the 1950s bull market is slightly different to the one I now use in the 1970s. You simply see what stops working and then use what does work.

To recap: The main theory always stays true and always will be. The mechanics of trading that theory will change from time to time.

The second question: Will you teach me how to trade?

First off: no. I am not a

teacher and it was never my intention to teach people how to trade successfully in the stock market. But you have everything you need in my three books to use my method. That's basically all one needs to use my method. Sure, it takes time and effort to really understand how to trade my way. But it's all there.

INTERVIEWER: I know what you mean, Nic. There are some "holes" in your books I am dying to ask you about. May I?

NIC: OK, go ahead.

INTERVIEWER: You say you never trade in a bear market. You only trade when the market has "the best chance of giving you a winning trade," and that is a bull market. How do you tell if the current market is a bull or a bear market?

NIC: Oh, that's really tricky and complicated. Not really. I simply look at a weekly chart of the averages over the past 6 months. If it's generally going down, it's a bear market. If it's going sideways or up I look for my stocks. It's as simple as that.

INTERVIEWER: That's it? Ha, ha...amazing. All those analysts spending hour after hour studying all kinds of economic reports, trends, forecasts, etc., and you simply look at the weekly chart. Shouldn't they simply do the same?

NIC: Probably. I too have to laugh at the way the markets work. Hey, they have to justify their jobs somehow. And if it means studying reports and writing forecasts - good for them. You'll always find the simplest of methods work the best. This is why I have never really studied fancy technical analysis. It simply doesn't make sense to me.

INTERVIEWER: What do you mean by "fancy technical analysis," Nic?

NIC: Well, you see, to me my method had to make sense. I had to be able to explain it to my partner (who knows absolutely nothing about stocks), and she had to grasp the reason why it worked. In short, it had to have a lot of common sense about it. My method was simply looking for the most in demand stocks, in the best sectors, in a market not going down. I would ride them as far as the ride would let me, and exit when it was over. Makes sense, right? But if you ask many traders to explain their method, straight away they mention waves, cycles, etc. My question is always: So WHY should a stock go up because of this? I am always left with a blank expression. They simply had no valid reason to trade these stocks. It had no common-sense reason to go up. And I found the most complicated technical analysis is like this. Great on theory, short in common sense.

Traders are much better spending their time on managing themselves and managing their money than trying to find a new "secret" to the markets.

INTERVIEWER: Talking of time. How long on average per day do you spend managing your trading account?

NIC: I religiously read Barron's every day. Well, not read it, but scan through it, and from this I can see the trend of the overall market, the leading sectors in that market, and the leading stocks. That's about all I need to know. This takes about 10 minutes. If I am in the market I then look at the quotes for my individual stocks to see if I need to move trailing stops. If I do, I will wire my broker with my new orders. This takes about another 10 minutes. That's about it.

INTERVIEWER: So on average, you manage your multi-million dollar portfolio in 20 minutes a day? Most mutual funds and some private investors will be shocked at this. Can you explain why they spend 8 hours+ a day managing their portfolios?

NIC: Well, it basically comes back to human psychology. A mutual fund managing many millions of dollars simply does not have the flexibility to jump in and out of most the momentum stocks. This is the single biggest advantage that most individual traders have over the large mutual funds.

You also have to realize the process that goes behind

managing stocks in a mutual fund. They cannot simply see a stock going up and buy it. They have to go through a whole process of and meetings with the management, shareholders, analysts. And this can mean buying a stock is a process that can take many weeks. Under this time, the stock and wealth advanced 10, 15, 20%+. This puts them at a huge disadvantage.

I'm not against mutual funds. I simply believe a good individual trader can easily outperform and do better for himself.

So to answer the question, the answer is simply about five to 10 minutes a day. I think any longer than this and it can actually be detrimental to your trading account.

INTERVIEWER: Nic, going through the book, "How I Made $2 Million in the Stock Market," it's quite obvious that you took some enormous risks early on in your trading career. I mean, at one stage, you are trading your whole account on 50% margin, and if it had have gone wrong it's safe to say you probably wouldn't be in the position you are in now. Some people might even say you got lucky. What would you say to that? How would you answer those critics?

NIC: Critics? You are talking about my trade in E.L. Bruce, right? What can I say? Sure, maybe in hindsight it was a bit of a gamble, but it sure paid off to the tune of $295,000. Everything seemed so right at that time. The markets were strong. The stock price and volume action was fantastic. I had made enormous profits in Lorillard and Diner's Club just previous to this trade. I figured if I placed a tight initial stop loss I would only be losing a small percentage of these profits.

The gamblers are the people who buy and hope. Sure, I traded big, but ONLY when all the right elements pieced together. I could easily go months without a trade. I even went two years without making a trade. I have no "need" to lose money in the stock market trading any old stock. It either hits me right in the face as a great trade or I ignore it.

And when I am wrong I get out with a small loss. I never let my losses get out of control. How is that "gambling" or being reckless?

INTERVIEWER: Would you class yourself as a trader or investor?

NIC: You tell me, what is classed as a trader or investor? There isn't one definition of this. By my definition, I am merely an investor. I look for "infant industries" to show me the strongest, most profitable stocks in those new industries.

I then wait for the "big boys" to work this out before I jump in for the ride.

INTERVIEWER: Infant industries - so not the strongest industries but infant industries. Why?

NIC: Think about it. My methods are nothing more than common sense. New industries is where the "expectation" is. It's new. People are always much more optimistic, excited by new industries. It's where the "hype" is, and most stocks trade not on what they have done but on what people "think" they will do in the future. A new industry has new money, new ideas, new hope. "It's different this time." Not for me is investing in radio, automobiles, T.V. They all had their spectacular runs. That's old news. I simply want to keep up with fashion.

INTERVIEWER: What about studying a company's earnings, revenues, products? What about tracking insiders buying and selling, etc.?

NIC: If you read my books, I state I always wanted to

trade in stocks with a fine past earning record. As far as studying fundamentals, that was ALL I was concerned with. Not that a stock having a fine past earnings history will help with the future advance. But most mutual funds followed these stocks. What interested me more was the potential or excitement about that stock. If it was an infant industry with a good past earnings record and the price and volume advances were right...it was a stock for me.

As for insiders... I don't concern

myself with their transactions. You will find insiders are just as prone to mistakes as the common trader. And I can tell everything I need to know about buyers and sellers by looking at the volume and price action of a stock. You can try to do too much in your trading. Often it will hinder your trading results rather then help them.

INTERVIEWER: You do mention in your latest book, Nic, "You Can Still Make It in the Stock Market," that your entry method changed a little after the success of your previous book,

"How I Made $2 Million in the Stock Market." Can you explain this in more detail?

NIC: Certainly. After my previous book sold over 500,000 copies, I guess all of the sudden there were something like one million investors all looking at the same kind of stock and looking for the same entry signal. This must have been a red flag to the floor traders who make a living from running the public's stop prices up. You could imagine orders in the tens of thousands for the same kind of stocks meant mass manipulation in the short term. My previous breakout methods were no longer working. I was getting whip-sawed all the time. When a method no longer works, change it. So I simply started buying stock AFTER the breakouts. This

worked. Nothing too difficult. I just had to wait a little longer for my entry point. Everything else stayed the same.

INTERVIEWER: Are you saying your original method is no longer valid? Do you regret publishing your book?

NIC: No, not at all to both counts. The method can never stop working. You may as well ask if the stock market has stopped working. My method IS how the stock markets work. If it stops working, the markets cease to exist. But the mechanics of entry and exit can and do change over time. As the masses flock to one entry method, it will get exploited by the floor traders and cease to work. Simply look for a small change in your entry and exit rules. You have to remember, most of the public are looking to be spoon-fed winners. They don't want to "think" about entry and exits. Use a method until it stops working. When it stops, ask yourself: "How can I get this method working again?" And then use it. You will have to make small changes every few years or so.

INTERVIEWER: So Nic, you are as successful now as you were in the late 1950s?

NIC: Yes. The markets aren't always quite so giving. We seem to now go through bear markets as often as we do go through bull markets. But I simply step out of bear markets and trade my kind of stocks in bull markets. They will ALWAYS be Darvas stock in the market. ALWAYS. By the way, a Darvas stock is a leading, high-priced active stock that can gain 100% in less than 6 months.

INTERVIEWER: OK, you got me. I was just about to ask you this. Do you go short in bear markets?

NIC: No. I simply keep out of bear markets and watch. I don't trade short, short-term, or dabble in low-priced stocks. I simply refuse to "lose" money unless it is in the pursuit of a Darvas stock.

INTERVIEWER: In a nutshell, your method would be:

Wait for a bull market cycle. Look at the leading industries. In those industries, look at the leading stocks. Follow those leading stock to see if they offer you an entry signal?

NIC: In a nutshell, yes, I would have to agree with this.

INTERVIEWER: Nic, when you seem

to have found it so easy to make a fortune in the stock market, why is it most cannot make it? It seems strange you make it seem so effortlessly easy, yet I'd say 99% of investors are losing money.

NIC: Well, just because I make money in the stock market, do not think it is easy for me. I too am prone to making mistakes. Even in this late stage, I wander off my method occasionally and lose money chasing some tip. We are all human and prone to mistakes. Don't forget, I too went through a five-year learning period from 1953 to 1958 where I lost a substantial amount of my capital before I worked out what worked and then was lucky enough to time it in the 1958-1960 bull market.

I get hundreds of letters every year from investors, and I can see the regular patterns to failure. The reasons are: They are not dedicated to one method. They gamble on tips, advice, and in low-priced stocks. They lack the discipline to stick to one method and wait for the very best opportunities.

Greed. They have not learned the basics of what good trading is.

Undercapitalized. They don't put the time and effort into really understanding how the markets and stocks work.

INTERVIEWER: OK, Nic. Thank you for this talk. Are you still investing?

NIC: Thank you. Yes, of course I am. Every day for about 10 minutes I scan the markets and manage my trades. It's become such a habit I doubt I'll ever stop. Every week I get excited by thinking there might just be another Darvas stock launching itself onto the launch pad. And that fills them with as much excitement now as it did way back in the 1950s. Thank you.

Recommended Readings

·Technical Analysis of Stock Trends,
Robert D. Edwards, John Magee,
www.bnpublishing.net

·Wall Street: The Other Las Vegas, Nicolas
Darvas, www.bnpublishing.net

·The Anatomy of Success, Nicolas Darvas,
www.bnpublishing.net

· The Dale Carnegie Course on Effective
Speaking, Personality Development, and
the Art of How to Win Friends & Influence
People, Dale Carnegie, www.bnpublishing.net

· The Law of Success In Sixteen Lessons by
Napoleon Hill (Complete, Unabridged),
Napoleon Hill, www.bnpublishing.net

· It Works, R. H. Jarrett,

www.bnpublishing.net

·Darvas System for Over the Counter Profits,

Nicolas Darvas, www.bnpublishing.net

· The Art of Public Speaking (Audio CD),

Dale Carnegie, wwww.bnpublishing.net

· The Success System That Never Fails

(Audio CD), W. Clement Stone,

www.bnpublishing.net

Breinigsville, PA USA
10 January 2010
230498BV00001B/23/P